An Eye on Spiders

Trapdoor Spiders

by Kristine Spanier

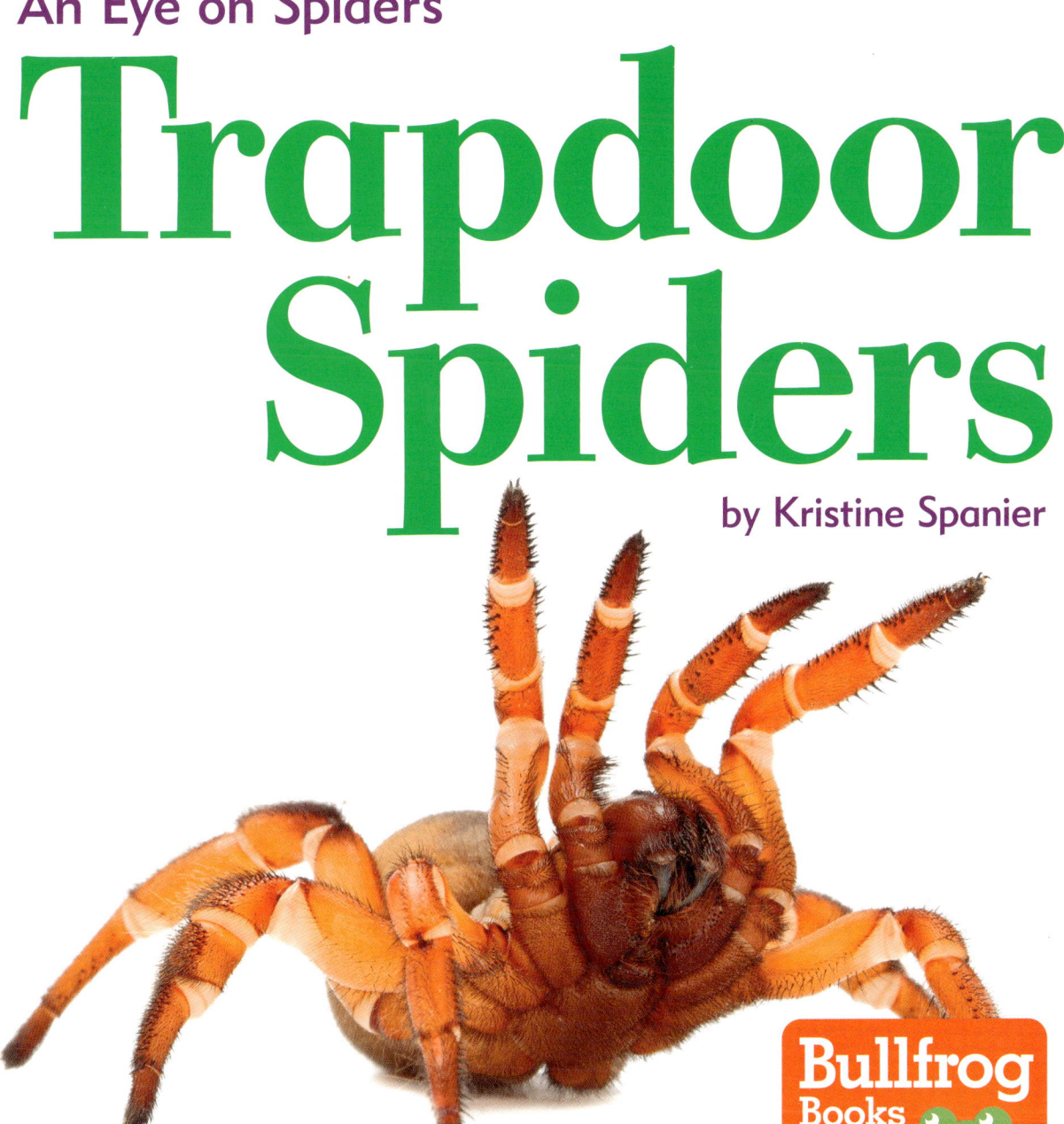

Bullfrog Books

Ideas for Parents and Teachers

Bullfrog Books let children practice reading informational text at the earliest reading levels. Repetition, familiar words, and photo labels support early readers.

Before Reading
- Discuss the cover photo. What does it tell them?
- Look at the picture glossary together. Read and discuss the words.

Read the Book
- "Walk" through the book and look at the photos. Let the child ask questions. Point out the photo labels.
- Read the book to the child, or have him or her read independently.

After Reading
- Prompt the child to think more. Ask: Have you seen the burrow of a trapdoor spider? What more would you like to learn about trapdoor spiders?

Bullfrog Books are published by Jump!
5357 Penn Avenue South
Minneapolis, MN 55419
www.jumplibrary.com

Copyright © 2019 Jump! International copyright reserved in all countries. No part of this book may be reproduced in any form without written permission from the publisher.

Library of Congress Cataloging-in-Publication Data

Names: Spanier, Kristine, author.
Title: Trapdoor spiders / by Kristine Spanier.
Description: Minneapolis, MN : Jump!, Inc., [2018]
Series: Bullfrog Books. An eye on spiders | "Bullfrog Books are published by Jump!"
Audience: Ages 5–8. | Audience: K to grade 3.
Includes bibliographical references and index.
Identifiers: LCCN 2017041193 (print)
LCCN 2017043180 (ebook)
ISBN 9781624967979 (e-book)
ISBN 9781624967962 (hardcover : alk. paper)
Subjects: LCSH: Spiders—Juvenile literature.
Spiders—Behavior—Juvenile literature.
Predation (Biology)—Juvenile literature.
Classification: LCC QL458.4 (ebook)
LCC QL458.4 .S6265 2018 (print) | DDC 595.4/4153—dc23
LC record available at https://lccn.loc.gov/2017041193

Editor: Jenna Trnka
Book Designer: Molly Ballanger

Photo Credits: blickwinkel/Alamy, cover; Biosphoto/Superstock, 1; Peter Waters/Shutterstock, 3, 24; Ingo Arndt/Nature Picture Library, 4; N A S./Science Source/Getty, 5 (left); anat chant/Shutterstock, 5 (right), James H Robinson/Science Source/Getty, 6–7, 23bl; Hans Christoph Kappel/Nature Picture Library, 8–9, 23tl; Pong Wira/Shutterstock, 10–11, 20–21; ardea.com/Mary Evans/Tonci/Pantheon/Superstock, 12; John Serrao/Photo Researchers/Biosphoto, 13, 23br; Barry Mansell/Nature Picture Library, 14–15; Nicky Bay/Flickr, 16–17, 18; Marc Anderson/Alamy, 19; Marco Maggesi/Shutterstock, 22; Matusciac Alexandru/Shutterstock, 23tr.

Printed in the United States of America at Corporate Graphics in North Mankato, Minnesota.

Table of Contents

Open. Grab. Shut!	4
Where in the World?	22
Picture Glossary	23
Index	24
To Learn More	24

Open. Grab. Shut!

A trap has been set.
Can you see it?

The bug does not see it.

Look out!
Open. Grab. Shut!
The spider is inside.
It has a good meal.

A trapdoor spider digs a hole.

It adds a door.

It makes a hinge with silk.

The door opens.

It closes.

The spider hides inside.

Trapdoor spiders are hairy.

hair

Some have markings.

marking

They are about one inch (2.5 centimeters) in size.

They are brown or black.

How long do they live?
Five to 20 years!

They like warm weather.
They live in forests.

They also live in deserts.

At night, the spider holds the door open.

It waits for prey.

It will be another good meal.

21

Where in the World?

Trapdoor spiders live in warm and tropical areas of Africa, China, Japan, North America, and South America.

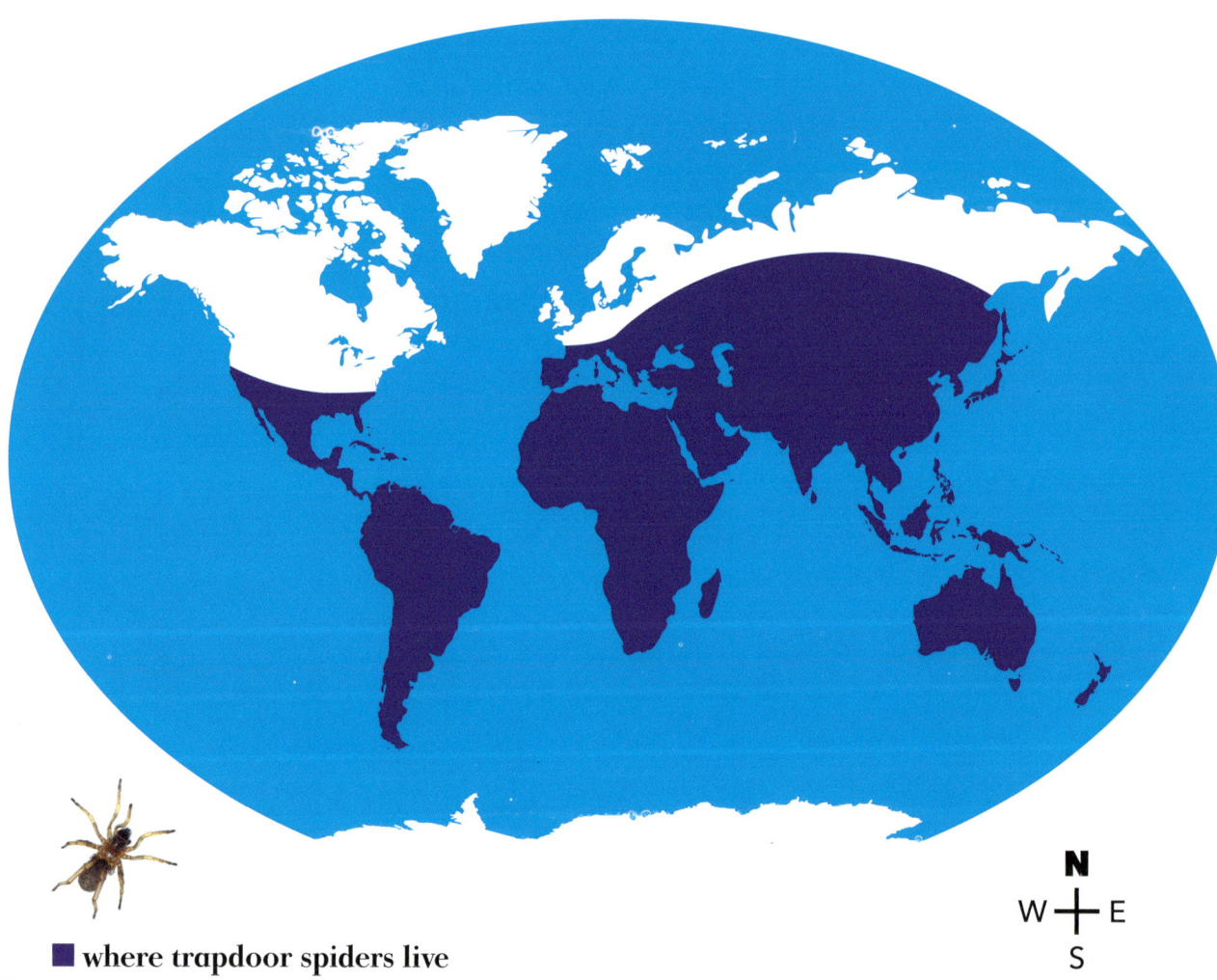

■ where trapdoor spiders live

Picture Glossary

hinge
A movable joint on which a door swings open and closed.

prey
An animal that is hunted by another animal for food.

markings
Patterns of marks.

silk
Fine fibers spiders make to build webs or nests.

Index

deserts 19
digs 9
door 9, 10, 20
forests 18
hairy 12
hinge 9
markings 13
meal 6, 20
prey 20
silk 9
size 14
trap 4

To Learn More

Learning more is as easy as 1, 2, 3.

1) Go to www.factsurfer.com

2) Enter "trapdoorspiders" into the search box.

3) Click the "Surf" button to see a list of websites.

With factsurfer.com, finding more information is just a click away.